# THE OFFICIAL CHELSEA FC ANNUAL 2018

Written by David Antill, Richard Godden,
James Sugrue and Dominic Bliss
Designed by Chris Dalrymple

A Grange Publication

©2017. Published by Grange Communications Ltd., Edinburgh, under licence from
Chelsea FC Merchandising Limited. www.chelseafc.com. Printed in the EU.

ISBN: 978-1-911287-68-1

# WELCOME TO THE OFFICIAL CHELSEA FC ANNUAL 2018!

Inside you will find everything you want to know about this year's squad, the incredible Premier League title-winning season in 2016/17 and much, much more.

We will reflect on our manager Antonio Conte's achievements, pay tribute to John Terry at the end of his remarkable Chelsea playing career and take a look at what makes PFA Player of the Year and FWA Footballer of the Year N'Golo Kanté so special.

We'll check in with Chelsea Ladies, who are looking to add more silverware to the collection this season. Let's not forget last year was also a great one for the Chelsea Academy, as our youth team won the treble!

Plus there's plenty of fun and games for you to get involved in, while we check out the best bits from our players' Instagram accounts, and don't miss your opportunity to win a signed shirt.

All in all, it promises to be a great read.

Enjoy!

STAMFORD AND BRIDGET

# CONTENTS

# CHAMPIONS!

Chelsea lift the trophy after being crowned Premier League champions.

# 2016/17 SEASON REVIEW

Chelsea started the season in dramatic fashion with Diego Costa scoring a late winner in a 2-1 victory over London rivals West Ham, meaning Antonio Conte's first competitive match in charge of the Blues ended with three points.

After defeats against Liverpool and Arsenal in September, it was time for a change for our trip to Hull when Conte switched to a three-man defence featuring Cesar Azpilicueta, Gary Cahill and David Luiz. Marcos Alonso and Victor Moses played as wing-backs and the new formation was an instant hit as we beat the Tigers 2-0.

Nobody knew then that it was the start of something special. We beat reigning champions Leicester 3-0 at the Bridge and then thrashed Manchester United 4-0, with Pedro scoring our quickest goal of the season after just 30 seconds!

Our match against Everton on Bonfire night started with fireworks and we produced exactly that on the pitch as we achieved our biggest win of the season, beating the Toffees 5-0. Two weeks later we won 1-0 against Middlesbrough and went top of the league for the first time, and that's where we stayed for the rest of the season.

Six more wins in December, which ended with a 4-2 victory over Stoke, made it 13 consecutive league victories for the Blues – a club record.

After nothing but wins in the league in October, November and December, Antonio Conte became the first person to win the Premier League Manager of the Month award three times in a row.

The New Year may have started with a defeat, but we were soon back on track with a 3-0 win at Leicester, including two goals from Marcos Alonso, and we also beat Brentford and Peterborough in the FA Cup.

February began with a 3-1 win against Arsenal, including Eden Hazard's unbelievable Goal of the Season (turn to page 40 for more on that). There was even a famous face in the dressing room afterwards – Hollywood actor Will Ferrell!

In March there were Premier League wins against West Ham and Stoke, but the standout result was our FA Cup quarter-final victory over Manchester United at the Bridge. N'Golo Kanté clearly likes playing against the Red Devils because he won the game with his second goal of the season – his first was also against them back in October.

April was always going to be a crunch month with seven fixtures for the Blues. After a couple of defeats – to Crystal Palace and Manchester United – we got back on track with a brilliant 4-2 victory over Spurs in the FA Cup semi-final at Wembley, followed by fantastic league wins against Southampton and Everton, with Gary Cahill scoring in both those games.

A 3-0 home win against Middlesbrough meant we could wrap up the title in a Friday night match at West Brom. It was a close encounter at the Hawthorns, but substitute Michy Batshuayi came off the bench to score a later winner and seal the title.

The league campaign finished with two home games against Watford and Sunderland. John Terry scored his final goal as a Chelsea player in a thrilling 4-3 win against the Hornets and we said goodbye to JT against the Black Cats, who we beat 5-1 on a day of celebration at Stamford Bridge, becoming the only team to achieve 30 Premier League wins in one season. Unbelievable!

# ANTONIO'S ANTICS

As soon as Antonio Conte arrived as Chelsea's first-team head coach, we were guaranteed to witness plenty of passion from the Italian on the touchline. Here are some of our favourite photos of him during and after games from our glorious 2016/17 season…

## STUNNING START

It didn't take long for Conte to get into the swing of things as Chelsea manager as he celebrated with the fans following our late win over West Ham at the start of the season.

## SURPRISE STRIKE

The gaffer enjoyed David Luiz's stunning free-kick at Liverpool as much as we did!

## MAN OF THE MOMENT

Celebrating with Eden Hazard after our FA Cup quarter-final win over Manchester United.

## TOFFEES TREASURE

Our 3-0 win at Everton at the end of April was a key victory and you can see what it meant to Conte.

## THE VIEW FROM ABOVE
If ever a photo captured what a goal means to Conte it's this one during our 3-1 win over Swansea.

## JOYOUS MOMENT
A season's worth of emotion pours out as Conte celebrates our win at West Brom which sealed the title.

## KING CONTE
Wearing a crown as he celebrates with the fans just after our 4-3 win over Watford…

## FLYING HIGH
… and being thrown in the air by his players to toast our title success.

## TROPHY TO TREASURE
Holding the Premier League trophy with John Terry after our 5-1 win on the final day against Sunderland.

# FAREWELL JT

After 22 years at the club, 19 of them as a first-team player, John Terry played his last game for Chelsea on the final day of last season. We take a look back at his incredible Blues career and that emotional farewell in May.

## MADE IN CHELSEA

In October 1998, in the 86th minute of a League Cup game against Aston Villa, a young defender from the Chelsea youth ranks came off the bench for his senior debut. His name was John Terry. He went on to make 717 appearances for the Blues – the third most in the club's history after Ron Harris and Peter Bonetti.

He initially joined the club as a 14-year-old, signing on the pitch at half-time of a game, but he worked very hard to make it to the first team, making sure he did extra work to show the manager and the other players that he was ready to step up.

"I cleaned the players' boots, as well as the dressing rooms, the toilets, the showers, even making coffee for players on the team bus," he recalled in his last-ever captain's notes for the matchday programme. "All of it was a great education and upbringing for me and I loved every minute of it. I had the hunger to become a regular first-team player and, ultimately, captain of our great club, and I'm so proud I did it."

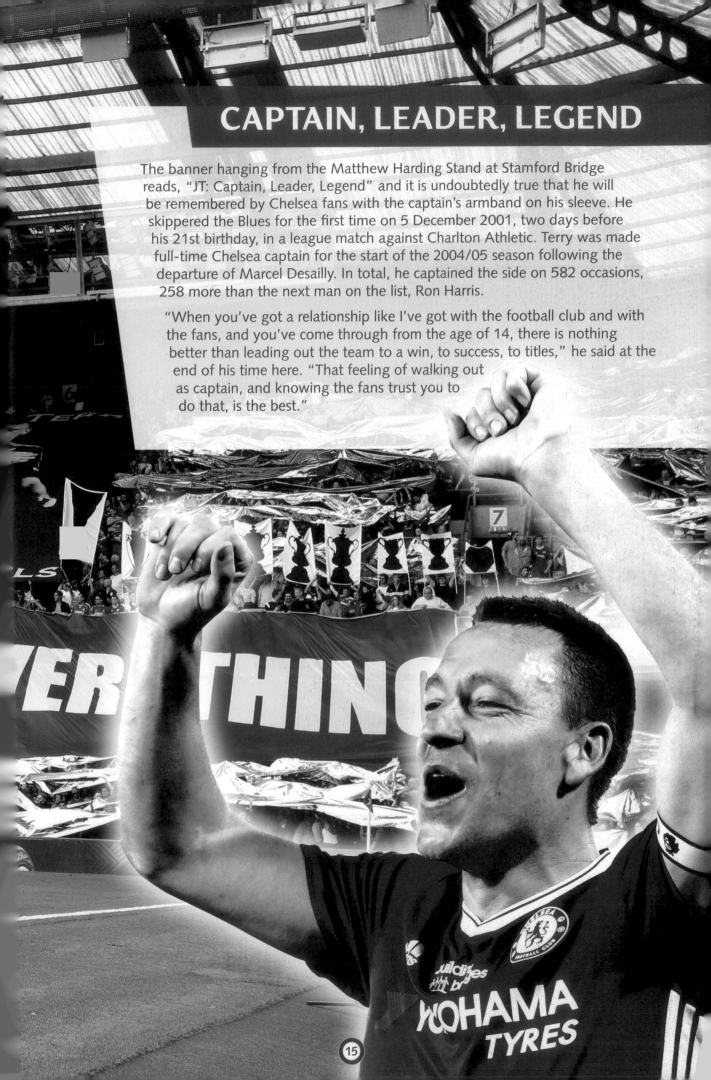

# CAPTAIN, LEADER, LEGEND

The banner hanging from the Matthew Harding Stand at Stamford Bridge reads, "JT: Captain, Leader, Legend" and it is undoubtedly true that he will be remembered by Chelsea fans with the captain's armband on his sleeve. He skippered the Blues for the first time on 5 December 2001, two days before his 21st birthday, in a league match against Charlton Athletic. Terry was made full-time Chelsea captain for the start of the 2004/05 season following the departure of Marcel Desailly. In total, he captained the side on 582 occasions, 258 more than the next man on the list, Ron Harris.

"When you've got a relationship like I've got with the football club and with the fans, and you've come through from the age of 14, there is nothing better than leading out the team to a win, to success, to titles," he said at the end of his time here. "That feeling of walking out as captain, and knowing the fans trust you to do that, is the best."

# TOP-SCORING DEFENDER

JT departed Chelsea as the highest-scoring defender we have ever had, with 67 goals – not bad for a centre-back! His best campaigns in front of goal were 2004/05 and 2014/15, when he banged in eight goals, so it's no surprise we won the league in both of those seasons. 41 of those goals came in the Premier League, making him the top-scoring defender since the division was rebranded in 1992. His goal against Watford in the penultimate game for the club ensured that he had scored in 17 consecutive Premier League seasons, the longest run by a defender. That was his last strike for Chelsea and it arrived over 17 years after his first – a header from a Gianfranco Zola corner in a 5-0 FA Cup win over Gillingham back in 2000.

# SHOW US YOUR MEDALS!

Terry is the most successful player in Chelsea's history. He has won the Premier League five times – in 2004/05, 2005/06, 2009/10, 2014/15 and 2016/17 – and is the only player to have captained a team to the title five times. He also has five FA Cup winner's medals to his name, having lifted the oldest trophy in world football in 2000, 2007, 2009, 2010 and 2012, and three League Cup winners' medals, from 2004/05, 2006/07 and 2014/15. As well as having all three major domestic trophies on his honours list, he has also won the two biggest European competitions, having lifted the Champions League trophy in 2012 and the Europa League trophy in 2013. Add his two Community Shield successes from 2005 and 2009 and that is some silverware collection!

# PLAYER PROFILES

## THIBAUT COURTOIS

Position: Goalkeeper
Date of birth: 11.05.1992
Nationality: Belgian
Signed from: Genk (July 2011)
Chelsea appearances: 108
Clean sheets: 39

**Did you know?**
Thibaut was a left-back when he joined the youth ranks of his first club, Genk. He played outfield until he was 11, when he decided he had a better future as a goalkeeper.

## EDUARDO

Position: Goalkeeper
Date of birth: 19.09.1982
Nationality: Portuguese
Signed from: Dinamo Zagreb (August 2016)
Chelsea appearances: 0
Clean sheets: 0

**Did you know?**
Eduardo is well travelled. He played league football in Portugal, Italy, Turkey and Croatia before joining Chelsea.

## WILLY CABALLERO

Position: Goalkeeper
Date of birth: 28.09.1981
Nationality: Argentinean
Signed from: Manchester City (July 2017)
Chelsea appearances: 0
Clean sheets: 0

**Did you know?**
Willy was part of the Argentina squad that won the gold medal for football at the 2004 Olympic Games.

## MARCOS ALONSO

Position: Defender
Date of birth: 28.12.1990
Nationality: Spanish
Signed from: Fiorentina (August 2016)
Chelsea appearances: 35
Goals: 6

**Did you know?**
Marcos comes from a long line of successful footballers. His dad played for Barcelona, Atletico Madrid and Spain, and his granddad won the European Cup five times with Real Madrid!

## ANDREAS CHRISTENSEN

Position: Defender
Date of birth: 10.04.1996
Nationality: Danish
Signed from: Brondby (February 2012)
Chelsea appearances: 3
Goals: 0

**Did you know?**
Andreas spent the last two seasons on loan at German club Borussia Monchengladbach, where he played in the Champions League and was named Player of the Year by the fans in 2015/16.

## CESAR AZPILICUETA
Position: Defender
Date of birth: 28.08.1989
Nationality: Spanish
Signed from: Marseille (August 2012)
Chelsea appearances: 228
Goals: 5

**Did you know?**
The defender played every single minute of every single Premier League game last season. He's only the fourth player to have done that for a title-winning team.

## GARY CAHILL
Position: Defender
Date of birth: 19.12.1985
Nationality: English
Signed from: Bolton Wanderers (January 2012)
Chelsea appearances: 239
Goals: 25

**Did you know?**
He might be a central defender but Gary scored eight times last season – the most in his career so far – taking his overall tally to 25 goals since he joined Chelsea.

## DAVID LUIZ
Position: Defender
Date of birth: 22.04.1987
Nationality: Brazilian
Signed from: Paris Saint-Germain (August 2016)
Chelsea appearances: 181
Goals: 13

**Did you know?**
David Luiz has now won the league three seasons in a row, after winning the French Ligue 1 with PSG in 2014/15 and 2015/16 and the Premier League with Chelsea in 2016/17.

## ANTONIO RÜDIGER
Position: Defender
Date of birth: 03.03.1993
Nationality: German
Signed from: Roma (July 2017)
Chelsea appearances: 0
Goals: 0

**Did you know?**
Antonio was part of the Germany squad who won the Confederations Cup in the summer of 2017.

## DAVIDE ZAPPACOSTA
Position: Defender
Date of birth: 11.06.1992
Nationality: Italian
Signed from: Torino (August 2017)
Chelsea appearances: 0
Goals: 0

**Did you know?**
Davide received his first call-up to the Italian national team from our very own Antonio Conte in May 2016, shortly before he became Chelsea manager.

# PLAYER PROFILES

## TIEMOUE BAKAYOKO

Position: Midfielder
Date of birth: 17.08.1994
Nationality: French
Signed from: Monaco
(July 2017)
Chelsea appearances: 0
Goals: 0

### Did you know?

Bakayoko's international debut for France was a tale of Chelsea midfielders past, present and future, as he was brought off the bench by former Blue Didier Deschamps to play alongside fellow Parisian Kanté. Their opponents Spain also had Pedro, Morata and Azpilicueta in their squad!

## VICTOR MOSES

Position: Midfielder
Date of birth: 12.12.1990
Nationality: Nigerian
Signed from: Wigan Athletic
(August 2012)
Chelsea appearances: 84
Goals: 14

### Did you know?

When he was at school, Victor's football coach was ex-Chelsea centre-back Colin Pates, who played over 300 games for the club in the 1980s.

## CESC FÀBREGAS

Position: Midfielder
Date of birth: 04.05.1987
Nationality: Spanish
Signed from: Barcelona (June 2014)
Chelsea appearances: 133
Goals: 18

### Did you know?

Last season Cesc Fàbregas became the only player ever to assist 10 or more Premier League goals in six different seasons.

## EDEN HAZARD

Position: Midfielder
Date of birth: 07.01.1991
Nationality: Belgian
Signed from: Lille (June 2012)
Chelsea appearances: 249
Goals: 72

### Did you know?

Eden Hazard is a big basketball fan and supports two-time NBA champions the New York Knicks, who he got to see play when they visited London for a match.

## N'GOLO KANTÉ

Position: Midfielder
Date of birth: 29.03.1991
Nationality: French
Signed from: Leicester City
(July 2016)
Chelsea appearances: 41
Goals: 2

**Did you know?**
N'Golo Kanté is the first outfield player to win back-to-back Premier League winner's medals with different clubs, sealing the title with Leicester in 2015/16 and Chelsea in 2016/17.

## KENEDY

Position: Midfielder
Date of birth: 08.02.1996
Nationality: Brazilian
Signed from: Fluminense
(August 2015)
Chelsea appearances: 23
Goals: 2

**Did you know?**
Kenedy's first start under Antonio Conte in 2016/17 was in a 4-3 win over Watford, the same club he spent the first half of the season on loan with.

## CHARLY MUSONDA

Position: Midfielder
Date of birth: 15.10.1996
Nationality: Belgian
Signed from: Anderlecht
(June 2012)
Chelsea appearances: 0
Goals: 0

**Did you know?**
Charly Musonda comes from a footballing family, with his father Charles being a Zambia international and brothers Lamisha, Tika and Matty all also having played in the Chelsea Academy.

## PEDRO

Position: Midfielder
Date of birth: 28.07.1987
Nationality: Spanish
Signed from: Barcelona
(August 2015)
Chelsea appearances: 83
Goals: 21

**Did you know?**
When Pedro started his career at Barcelona he wore the name Pedrito on his shirt, which means "Little Pedro" in his native Spanish language.

## WILLIAN

Position: Midfielder
Date of birth: 09.08.1988
Nationality: Brazilian
Signed from: Anzhi
Makhachkala (August 2013)
Chelsea appearances: 181
Goals: 31

**Did you know?**
Willian's first goals at Stamford Bridge came against Chelsea, scoring twice for Shakhtar Donetsk in a 3-2 win for the Blues in the 2012/13 Champions League group stage.

## DANNY DRINKWATER

Position: Midfielder
Date of birth: 05.03.1990
Nationality: English
Signed from: Leicester City
(August 2017)
Chelsea appearances: 0
Goals: 0

**Did you know?**
Danny won the Premier League title with Leicester City in 2015/16, when he was playing alongside none other than N'Golo Kanté in the centre of midfield.

## MICHY BATSHUAYI

Position: Forward
Date of birth: 02.10.1993
Nationality: Belgian
Signed from: Marseille (July 2016)
Chelsea appearances: 28
Goals: 9

**Did you know?**
Fans in Belgium have given Michy Batshuayi superhero status by nicknaming him "Batsman" due to his similar name and habit of scoring big goals.

## ALVARO MORATA

Position: Forward
Date of birth: 23.10.1992
Nationality: Spanish
Signed from: Real Madrid (July 2017)
Chelsea appearances: 0
Goals: 0

**Did you know?**
Morata has played in three of the last four Champions League finals, winning the competition with Real Madrid in 2014 and 2017, as well as being on the losing side for Juventus in 2015.

## DIEGO COSTA

Position: Forward
Date of birth: 07.10.1988
Nationality: Spanish
Signed from: Atletico Madrid
(July 2014)
Chelsea appearances: 120
Goals: 59

**Did you know?**
Although Diego Costa was born and raised in Brazil, he has represented Spain at international level.

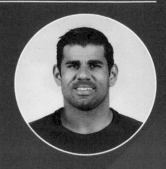

# WE ARE THE PRIDE

THE NEW 2017/18 CHELSEA FC NIKE KIT

## JOIN US AT NIKE.COM/CHELSEA

# PICTURE PERFECT

Plenty of Chelsea's first-team squad are active on Instagram, sharing photographs and videos to give supporters an insight into what life is like to play for the Blues. Here are a few of our favourite images, along with an explanation from the player in the photograph.

### Marcos Alonso

"We have been going out for dinner once a month all together as a group, just enjoying each other's company off the pitch as well. It's been a great help and the atmosphere within the squad is amazing. You can see that when we're on the pitch. It's organised by the manager and the captain and it's good fun for everyone."

### Pedro

"This photo was taken at a water park in Tenerife which is very famous across Europe. I was there with my family, we go there every year during the summer holidays and I really like this picture, which is me with one of the sea lions."

## Willian

"This is my wife, I'm always with her. This photo was taken in the summer, we were enjoying the weather in London and acting like tourists. We had some friends with us on this day and it's good, when you have a few days off, to have a look around the city. This was a lovely day so it was perfect for us. I really enjoy London and I try to go out for dinner, or to different places, when I can. Family is very important for me."

## Thibaut Courtois

"I love sports in general and I enjoy watching the NBA and NFL. I'm probably a bigger basketball fan but the Super Bowl is a unique event and it's not easy to get to because it's played when we are in the middle of our season. It was lucky we had three days off around that time so I was able to travel and see some NBA and watch the Super Bowl. It was an amazing experience and an amazing game."

## Eden Hazard

"It's not often my family are all together so when we are we have to do something entertaining. In this picture I'm playing Monopoly with my three brothers, Thorgan, Kylian and Ethan. We get on very well and they all play football. Thorgan is in Germany, Kylian plays in Budapest and Ethan plays for a local team."

# HOME & AWAY

These Chelsea players tell us about the country they come from, the places they have travelled to during their football careers and where they would like to visit in the future...

### N'GOLO KANTE

The first time I left France would have been when I went on holiday to Mali for about two months to visit my family. I was about 11 and it was very exciting. I got to meet a lot of my family too.

### DAVID LUIZ

Brazil is defined firstly by happiness, then I would say solidarity and the fact our culture is very accepting. We accept everybody and try to help them.

### THIBAUT COURTOIS

I'd like to go to Australia or Thailand in the future. It's a shame I haven't had the chance to visit yet because there are such nice cities and beaches. The wildlife in Australia is particularly impressive – I'd love to see some kangaroos!

## MARCOS ALONSO

There are a lot of sportsmen in Spain who are very good. In Formula One Fernando Alonso has been champion a few times, we have a good basketball team and in tennis we have Rafa Nadal, so all of those sports are very popular as well as football.

## GARY CAHILL

I'd have to say my favourite places in the world are America and Dubai. If I had to pick a city in the US it would be New York because there's so much to do, so much going on, and the people have a really good attitude to life.

## CESAR AZPILICUETA

My hometown, Pamplona, is where I was born and where I lived for many years. It is a small town. Wherever you go in the street, you know the people you see, or you know their brother or their friend. In some way, you know everyone and everyone knows you.

## EDEN HAZARD

I've been to a lot of places for football. I went to Brazil for the 2014 World Cup but I would like to go to other parts of South America like Argentina and Chile, it would be nice to go to Mexico as well.

# BACKLINE BUDDIES

Gary Cahill and David Luiz formed a vital part of the Chelsea defence last season and they also showed they are great mates off the pitch when they appeared at the club's An Audience With event alongside former Blues full-back Paulo Ferreira. Here are some of the highlights from an entertaining evening at Stamford Bridge.

## WHO IS THE BEST STRIKER YOU HAVE PLAYED AGAINST?

David Luiz (DL): Messi

Gary Cahill (GC): Ronaldo

Paulo Ferreira (PF): I have to say Didier Drogba. I played against him in the Champions League when he was at Marseille and I was at Porto.

## WHAT ARE THE TRAINING SESSIONS LIKE UNDER ANTONIO CONTE?

GC: Hard.

DL: Very hard!

## IS HE THE SAME ON THE TRAINING FIELD AS HE IS ON THE TOUCHLINE, WITH THE PASSION HE SHOWS?

DL: He's the same with everything – when you're training, when you go for something to eat! I'm just joking, he is an amazing coach.

GC: The way we work is really intense. We do a lot of physical training, a lot of tactical training.

## HOW IS ANTONIO MAKING YOU A BETTER PLAYER?

DL: I think it is just through the work. That's why we are improving game by game, day by day, because we really work hard every day. It is not a secret, if you want to win things, you must work.

GC: It's true, working hard comes first and foremost. You've seen him on the side of the pitch and he is very similar to that in person. He comes across as a guy who is constantly thinking about the game, constantly thinking about how he can do things different or better and that rubs off on us.

## DAVID, BOTH YOUR PARENTS ARE TEACHERS SO YOU HAD TO BE GOOD ACADEMICALLY, EVEN AS A TEENAGE FOOTBALLER. WHAT WERE YOUR FAVOURITE SUBJECTS AT SCHOOL?

DL: Mathematics – I love numbers.

GC: It would have to be PE for me. Second to that was probably English, although David says he never understands any of my English. I think it must be the Yorkshire accent!

# CHELSEA HISTORY: DOUBLE CUP JOY FOR BLUES

**The 2017/18 campaign marks the 20th anniversary of a memorable season for Chelsea, when we won a major domestic trophy as well as triumphing in Europe.**

This might not sound all that amazing when you consider the amount of success the Blues have achieved in recent years, but two decades ago we were not used to lifting silverware so regularly.

Having won the FA Cup in 1997 – our first major honour in 26 years – by beating Middlesbrough 2-0, we faced the same opposition in the 1998 League Cup final and won by the same scoreline. Gianluca Vialli took on the player-manager role just before the second leg of our semi-final tie against Arsenal, which we won 3-1 to reach Wembley.

The final went to extra time after no goals inside 90 minutes, with defender Frank Sinclair netting the opener early in extra time before Italian midfielder Roberto Di Matteo – who scored inside the first minute in the '97 final – sealed the victory.

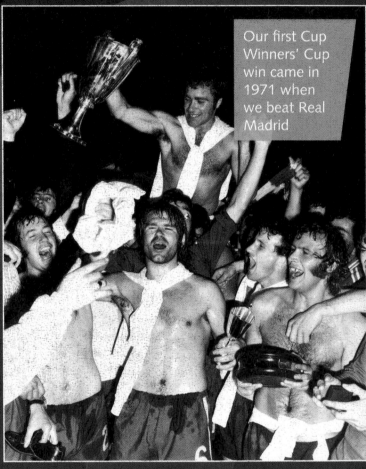

Our first Cup Winners' Cup win came in 1971 when we beat Real Madrid

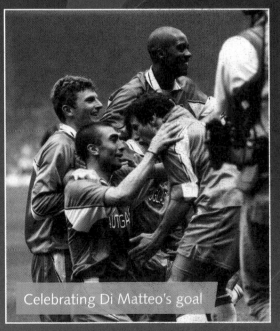

Celebrating Di Matteo's goal

The Chelsea team lines up before the final at Wembley

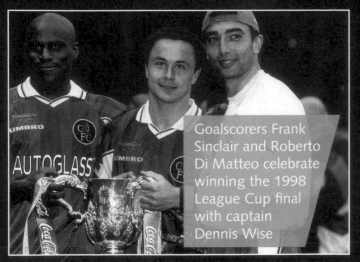

Goalscorers Frank Sinclair and Roberto Di Matteo celebrate winning the 1998 League Cup final with captain Dennis Wise

It was our second success in that competition – having first won it in 1965 – and we also made it two European Cup Winners' Cup victories a couple of months later. Our run to the final included a famous game in Norway against Tromso, which was played in heavy snow.

The final took place in Swedish capital city Stockholm against Stuttgart and the only goal came from one of our greatest players of all time, Gianfranco Zola, who had only been on the pitch for 30 seconds before scoring with practically his first touch.

We also won the Cup Winners' Cup in 1971, when a much-loved Chelsea side beat the great Real Madrid in Athens.

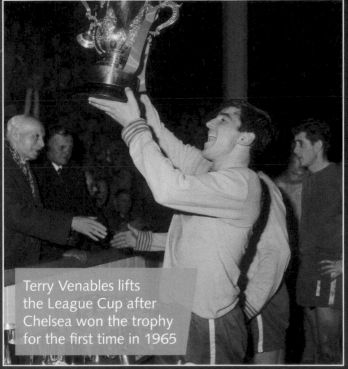

Terry Venables lifts the League Cup after Chelsea won the trophy for the first time in 1965

Our game against Tromso in Norway took place in thick snow

Gianfranco Zola nets our winner in the 1998 European Cup Winners' Cup final against Stuttgart and reels away to celebrate

Zola proudly holds the trophy with player-manager Gianluca Vialli

Joyous scenes for the whole team

# 24 GARY CAHILL
## POSITION: DEFENDER

# 9 ALVARO MORATA
## POSITION: STRIKER

# INSIDER

Just because the players are working hard at Cobham every day to get in top shape to win football matches, it doesn't mean they can't also have a little fun. Here are some of the best bits behind the scenes with the Blues.

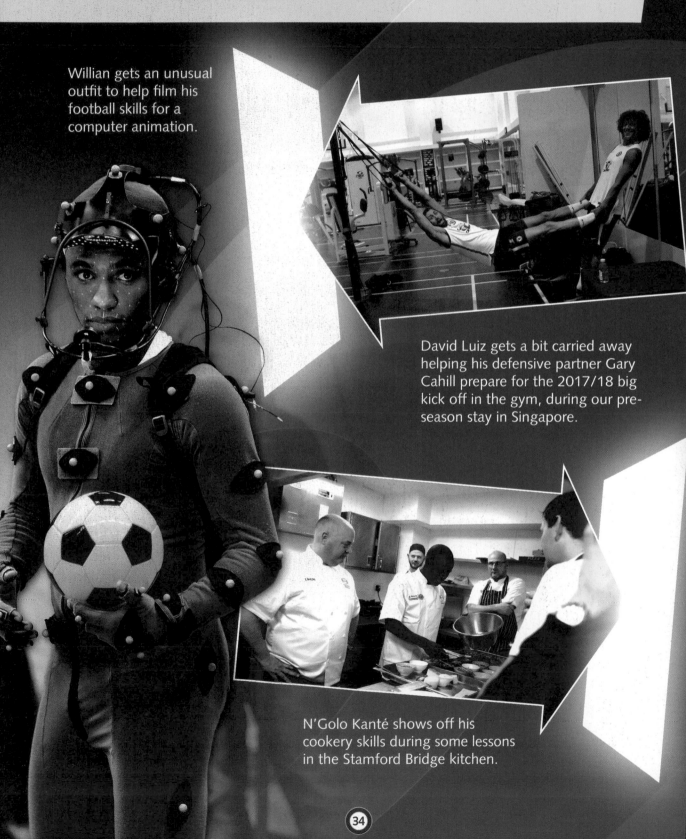

Willian gets an unusual outfit to help film his football skills for a computer animation.

David Luiz gets a bit carried away helping his defensive partner Gary Cahill prepare for the 2017/18 big kick off in the gym, during our pre-season stay in Singapore.

N'Golo Kanté shows off his cookery skills during some lessons in the Stamford Bridge kitchen.

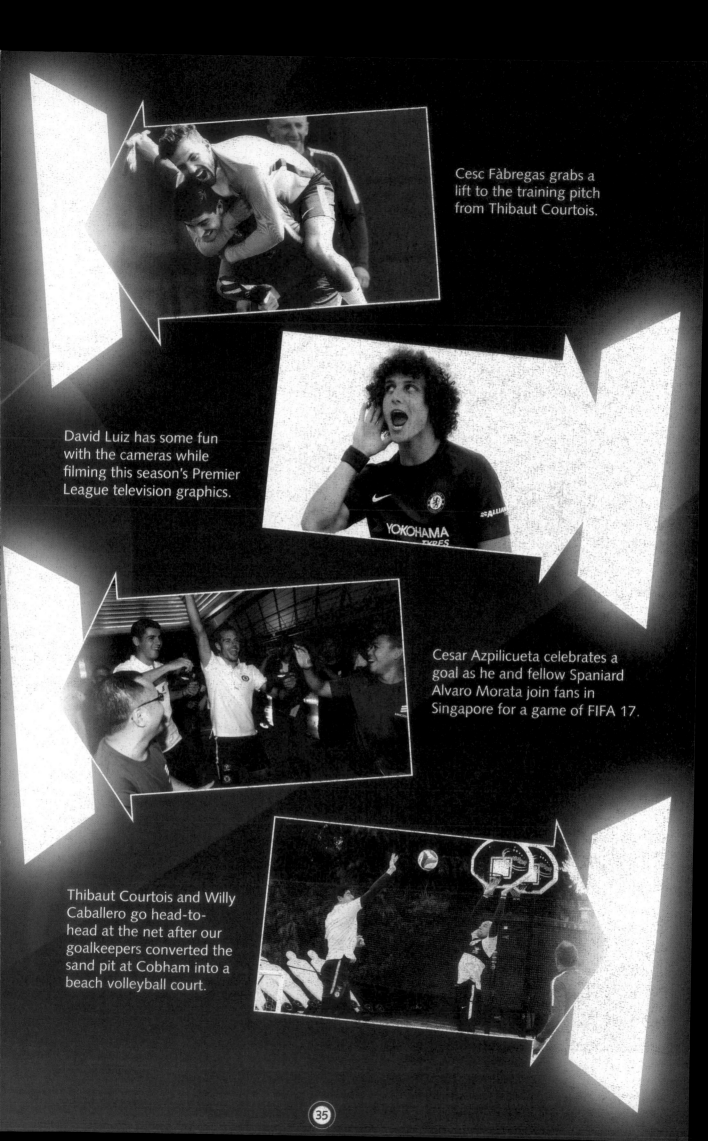

Cesc Fàbregas grabs a lift to the training pitch from Thibaut Courtois.

David Luiz has some fun with the cameras while filming this season's Premier League television graphics.

Cesar Azpilicueta celebrates a goal as he and fellow Spaniard Alvaro Morata join fans in Singapore for a game of FIFA 17.

Thibaut Courtois and Willy Caballero go head-to-head at the net after our goalkeepers converted the sand pit at Cobham into a beach volleyball court.

# ACADEMY
## TREBLE CHAMPIONS!

Chelsea's Academy has enjoyed more than its fair share of success in the last few years, but the 2016/17 campaign was up there as one of the very best. The Under-18s team – coached by former Blues midfielder Jody Morris – won the treble last season, taking the southern section league title in February, then winning the Under-18 Premier League for the first time, and retaining the FA Youth Cup for a fourth year in a row. Let's take a look back at how they did it.

# THE FA YOUT

# CUP KINGS

Chelsea have now won the FA Youth Cup six times in the last eight years, and we were runners-up once in that time as well. It's an incredible sign of the strength of our youth teams in the last decade.

In last season's final we beat Manchester City 6-2 on aggregate after drawing the away leg 1-1, then winning the home leg 5-1. It was the third year running we have beaten City in the final and this was the biggest victory of them all. Antonio Conte was at Stamford Bridge for the home leg of the final and youth-team captain Mason Mount admitted that they got an extra buzz from knowing that the boss was watching.

"It gives us a lot of confidence to see Antonio Conte here watching us," he said after the game. "We are all good players who want to progress further and move up through the club. We're very happy to be able to show what we can do on these big occasions. There is a winning mentality in the Academy and we are brought up to have that as young players."

## THE FINAL

### FIRST LEG

Man City 1
Foden

Chelsea 1
Ugbo

Chelsea (3-4-3): Thompson; James, T Chalobah, Guehi; Sterling, Maddox, Uwakwe (Gallagher 90+1), Castillo; Mount (c), Ugbo (St Clair 87), Hudson-Odoi

### SECOND LEG

Chelsea 5
T Chalobah, Ugbo, Hudson-Odoi, Sterling, C Dasilva

Manchester City 1
Nmecha

Chelsea (3-4-3): Cumming; James, T Chalobah, Guehi; Sterling, Maddox, Uwakwe (McEachran 81), Castillo; Mount (c), Ugbo (Taylor-Crossdale 78), Hudson-Odoi (C Dasilva 84)

# CHELSEA'S FA YOUTH CUP TRIUMPHS

*Aggregate results given for all finals*

1959/60: CHELSEA 5 PRESTON NORTH END 2

1960/61: CHELSEA 5 EVERTON 3

2009/10: CHELSEA 3 ASTON VILLA 2

2011/12: CHELSEA 4 BLACKBURN ROVERS 1

2013/14: CHELSEA 7 FULHAM 6

2014/15: CHELSEA 5 MANCHESTER CITY 2

2015/16: CHELSEA 4 MANCHESTER CITY 2

2016/17: CHELSEA 6 MANCHESTER CITY 2

Legendary Chelsea youth-team coach, Dick Foss, holds the FA Youth Cup that his teams won in 1959/60 and 1960/61. A great servant to the club, Foss had previously made 48 first-team appearances for Chelsea in a playing career that was interrupted by the Second World War.

# CHELSEA CHAMPIONS

We also won the Under-18 Premier League in 2016/17, making sure our youth team were completely dominant last season. The league season was divided into two sections and began with a regional league, the southern section, with 12 teams from the south of England competing. We finished top of the southern section for the third season in a row and progressed to the elite stage of the league, where the best eight youth teams in the country came up against each other for the title.

In the end, Chelsea beat six of our seven opponents, losing just one game, and therefore finished the season as champions of England, just like the first team. It was the first time our youth team had won the league since 1984. With the southern section and the FA Youth Cup to our name as well, the treble was complete.

"It's been an amazing season for us," said the team's proud coach, Jody Morris, at the end of it all. "We've broken records and won every competition we've entered, so I couldn't be prouder of the lads."

# GOALS GALORE

Chelsea's youth team scored their fair share of goals in 2016/17. At the end of the southern section in February, our Under-18s had bagged 68 goals – 17 more than the next highest in the region. The most striking result of all was a 13-0 win over Brighton, and at the end of that Jody Morris said we could have scored even more. That's a coach with high standards!

Meanwhile, young Blues striker Martell Taylor-Crossdale finished as the league's top scorer by a comfortable margin, with 20 goals to his name.

However, the team also showed its steely side as we conceded the fewest goals in both the southern section and the elite section. In fact, we kept 17 clean sheets in the league alone last season. It came down to great talent, hard work and an unbeatable team spirit.

"It's been a massive team effort because we've worked really hard in training," said defender Josh Grant, one of the more experienced heads in the group last season. "We've made history again because nobody has ever achieved this before. We have a great group of lads who've been playing together for a long time now and there's definitely nobody else I'd rather share these moments with."

# SIZZLING STRIKES

Not many people would argue with the winner of Chelsea's Goal of the Season in 2016/17 as Eden Hazard claimed that honour for the second time thanks to his stunning solo effort against Arsenal. We look back on Hazard's wonder goal – where he ran from his own half, took on four defenders before finishing beautifully – and a few other worldies from our triumphant campaign.

GOAL

Cesar Azpilicueta scored a sensational volley in our League Cup win over Leicester.

N'Golo Kanté's only two goals in 2016/17 came against Manchester United – his brilliant run and tidy finish in the 4-0 home win over the Red Devils was one of our best of the season.

Pedro had three stunning strikes in our Goal of the Season shortlist, including a wonderful curling effort in our 2-1 victory over Spurs.

David Luiz was a rock at the back all season but he also showed he still had an eye for the spectacular with his surprise free-kick against Liverpool at Anfield, which certainly impressed the gaffer!

Marcos Alonso scored an impressive six goals in his debut season as a Blue, with the Spaniard's free-kick at Bournemouth the pick of the bunch.

Nemanja Matic chose the best possible stage for a 30-yard wonder goal, netting our fourth in the 4-2 win over Spurs in the FA Cup semi-final at Wembley.

# CHELSEA'S SPANISH SET

Chelsea may be a high-tempo Premier League side, with an Italian master as our manager, but there is no denying the strong Spanish influence in our team.

In Cesar Azpilicueta, Cesc Fàbregas, Marcos Alonso, Pedro and Alvaro Morata, we have a collection of top talent from Spain, and each one brings something different to the side.

## FÀBREGAS IS MAGIC

The man in the magic hat is also the king of the assist. Between his arrival at Stamford Bridge in the summer of 2014 and the end of last season, when he won the league with Chelsea for the second time, no Premier League player made more assists than Cesc, who managed 37 in that period. At the end of last season, he had set up the second-highest number of goals since the Premier League began, with 107. Cesc's eye for a pass makes him one of the most deadly players in the world when it comes to unlocking a tight game. Never rule us out while the man from Catalonia is on the pitch.

## ALL HAIL CESAR

He may come from Pamplona, where every year the local people set a bull loose in the streets as part of a festival, but you will never see Cesar Azpilicueta taking risks like that on the football pitch. Last season, Chelsea's Mr Reliable played every single minute of every Premier League game as we won the title. Azpi has also proved he can play anywhere across the back. He signed for Chelsea as a right-back, then switched to left-back and, last season, he found a new home as one of our three centre-backs. Incredibly, when he first started out as a 17-year-old with his local club Osasuna, he was a right-winger!

## PACEY PEDRO

Few players have won more than Pedro, who has tasted success in the World Cup, the European Championships, the Champions League, as well as the league title in Spain and England. The rapid winger grew up on the sunny island of Tenerife, so it's no surprise that he always plays with a smile on his face. He says the friendship between our Spanish players is great for team spirit.

"I think away from the pitch we have a good relationship. We all get on very well and that has built our confidence. Spending time together and having a good friendship has converted into a good relationship on the pitch as well."

## OH! MARCOS ALONSO!

Marcos Alonso had a fantastic first season at Chelsea. After signing from Italian club Fiorentina he became our first-choice left wing-back as we won the Premier League – his first piece of silverware. He comes from a famous football family in Spain. His grandfather and his father are both called Marcos Alonso as well and they played at the highest level for club and country. His granddad won the European Cup (the original name for the Champions League) five times with Real Madrid in the 1950s and his dad played for Barcelona and Atletico Madrid.

## MARVELLOUS MORATA

A new arrival at Stamford Bridge at the start of this season, Alvaro Morata has already starred on the very biggest stages in world football. The Spain international striker, who scored a fantastic header against Burnley in his Premier League debut in August, has previously played for Real Madrid and Juventus, winning the league and cup multiple times in both Spain and Italy. He has also been part of two Champions League-winning squads with Real Madrid and scored in another Champions League final with Juventus in 2015, although he ended up on the losing side on that occasion. With that kind of winning experience behind him, he could certainly prove an important player for the Blues when it comes to crunch time at the end of the season.

# CHELSEA DISCO

Just like the teacher at a school disco, the Chelsea players have some pretty embarrassing dance moves. The good news is they are practising, the bad news is they are still so bad Antonio Conte can't even watch...

Victor Moses at least has his acrobatics working for him, thanks to his signature somersault.

Moses is also part of the Blues' line dancing group, but it looks like they're struggling to teach him to stay in routine.

Despite getting some ballroom practice in the gym, Azpi still doesn't look ready to lead.

David Luiz is going down a different route, practising some ballet poses.

Gary Cahill gets lifted up for the big finishing move, but unfortunately it still seems to take the whole team to do it.

# CHELSEA LADIES

Chelsea Ladies are the team to beat once again in the FA Women's Super League after winning the Spring Series trophy at the end of a shortened eight-game season in 2017. Women's football in England now reverts to a winter league, having been played in the summer since 2011. We bring you up to speed with everything you need to know about Emma Hayes' trophy-winning Blues squad.

## FA WSL SPRING SERIES WINNERS 2017

The Blues dazzled the WSL across the course of the eight-match campaign, sprinting out of the blocks and, after a slight wobble in the middle, holding their nerve to seal a deserved title with a 2-0 win at Birmingham. We scored 32 times, which was 10 more goals than any other side, at an average of four per game, conceded the fewest as our net was breached only three times, and ended with a goal difference that was 15 higher than the next best. There could be no doubt it was a deserved triumph as we celebrated a third trophy in two years.

## PLAYER OF THE YEAR: KAREN CARNEY

It's safe to say 2017 has been a pretty good year for Chelsea's England international midfielder. She woke up on the last day of 2016 to find out she had been awarded an MBE by the Queen, an honour which had previously been bestowed upon Emma Hayes, and a trip to Buckingham Palace followed for Carney. Then, in the space of a month or so, she had been named Chelsea Ladies Player of the Year and scored the winning goal as we clinched the Spring Series!

## SPRING SERIES GOLDEN BOOT: FRAN KIRBY

Having been out of action for more or less a whole year, we would have forgiven the former Reading star a gentle return to first-team football. What followed in the final fortnight of the season was nothing short of remarkable: six goals at a rate of one every 40 minutes, which secured the Golden Boot for Kirby. There is no deadlier finisher in the English game!

## CONTE MEETS HAYES

A strong defence was crucial for the Ladies in 2017 and a back three proved to be just as good for them as it had for the men's team. Emma Hayes was able to compare notes with Antonio Conte when they met up at the training ground.

## NEED TO KNOW:

Kirby is an absolute ledge off the pitch as well as on it. She found out that seven-year-old Blues fan Isla Turner had "Kirby 14" on the back of her Chelsea shirt when she scored a penalty past Stamford the Lion at the Bridge, so Fran popped in to visit Isla a few weeks later with some signed goodies and for a quick kickabout!

## CLAIRE RAFFERTY

Claire Rafferty is the Ladies' longest-serving player and in the summer of 2017 she celebrated her 10th anniversary as a Blue. As well as being a quality left-back, Raff is also a great role model and she joined our global charity partner Plan International in Colombia last summer as part of their Champions of Change campaign. You can also read her blogs on the official Blues website.

## DEANNA COOPER

Deanna Cooper was playing for London Bees in WSL 2 when Emma Hayes spotted her. A few months later she was one of the stars of the Spring Series after an excellent campaign as part of our stingy back three, but that wasn't the biggest surprise when it comes to Deanna: she is also a brilliant cricketer and has played for England at junior level!

History was made in October 2016 when Chelsea Ladies played their first competitive game at Stamford Bridge. Wolfsburg were the opponents for a Women's Champions League match and the Germans, who have won the competition twice in recent years, proved to be too strong for the Blues.

Erin Cuthbert, Crystal Dunn, Maren Mjelde and Ramona Bachmann entertained fans at Stamford Bridge during An Audience With... Keep your eyes peeled for news of further events involving the Ladies.

## KINGSMEADOW

Chelsea Ladies have a new home! Having spent the past five years at Wheatsheaf Park, the Blues moved into Kingsmeadow, which is in nearby Kingston-upon-Thames, ahead of the 2017/18 season. Tickets cost £3 for kids and £6 for adults. You can find more information on chelseafc.com.

**Keep up to date with the Chelsea Ladies via their Twitter page, @ChelseaLFC.**

All membership tiers include priority access to match tickets

# JUNIOR MEMBERSHIP 2017/18

On sale now

**CHELSEAFC.COM/MEMBERSHIP**

# WHEN WE WERE YOUNG

Just for fun, see how many Chelsea players you can recognise from these photos of earlier in their football careers...

A _____

B _____

C _____

D _____

E _____

F _____

Answers on page 61

# CAPTAIN, LEADER, QUIZMASTER!

John Terry left Chelsea last summer after an unforgettable 22 years at Stamford Bridge. He will forever be remembered as one of our greatest-ever players, so you need to make sure you are clued up when it comes to the man known as Captain, Leader, Legend...

**Q1**

Who was the manager of Chelsea when John Terry made his debut against Aston Villa in a League Cup game in 1998?

a) Ruud Gullit   b) Claudio Ranieri   c) Gianluca Vialli

**Q2**

Terry's middle name is the same as the given name for which member of the royal family?

a) Charles   b) George   c) William

**Q3**

Who played more games for Chelsea alongside JT than any other player?

a) Ashley Cole   b) Didier Drogba   c) Frank Lampard

**Q4**

Here are Chelsea's four most successful captains of all time (from left to right: Dennis Wise, Ron Harris, Roy Bentley and Terry). Other than John Terry, who is the only one to have skippered the Blues to a league title?

a) Bentley   b) Harris   c) Wise

## Q5

Derbies were a big deal to the London-born centre-half. Against which local rival did he score more of his 67 Chelsea goals against than any other side?

a) Arsenal   b) Charlton Athletic   c) Fulham

## Q6

Speaking of London-born, in which part of the capital was JT born and raised? It shares its name with a noise made by a dog!

a) Barking   b) Growling   c) Woofing

## Q7

This image hasn't been photoshopped – Terry really did play as a goalkeeper for Chelsea in a game against Reading in 2006. Why did he stand-in between the sticks for the Blues?

a) Ashley Cole dared him   b) He represented England at youth level as a goalkeeper
c) Both our goalies were injured

## Q8

JT is a quality pool player, but who won when he took on snooker's World Champion, Neil Robertson, who is a massive Chelsea fan, in a game at the Cobham training ground?

a) JT   b) It was a draw   c) Robertson

## Q9

JT netted his only cup final goal to help us beat Spurs at Wembley in the League Cup final in 2015. Can you spot the ball?

## Q10

Terry joined Aston Villa after leaving the Blues, but it wasn't his first spell in the second tier of English football. Which club did he represent, on loan, in 2000?

a) Derby County
b) Nottingham Forest
c) Preston North End

Answers on page 61

# THREE INTO ONE

We've jumbled up the faces of some Chelsea stars. Can you tell who the three Blues players are in each of these pictures?

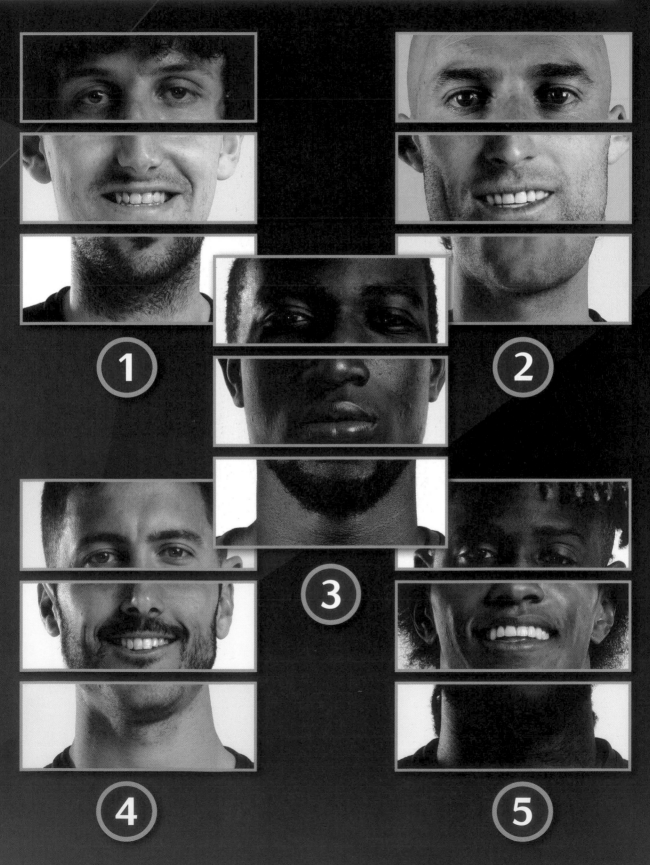

Answers on page 61

# HERE, THERE AND EVERYWHERE: N'GOLO KANTÉ

What a year it has been for N'Golo Kanté! He became the first outfield player to win back-to-back Premier League winner's medals with different clubs, having also lifted the trophy in 2016 with Leicester City. The Frenchman celebrated with a hat-trick of personal honours after being selected as Player of the Year by the Premier League, PFA and Football Writers' Association. Here are some of the stats and stories behind his incredible rise…

Kanté only became a professional footballer five years ago and his earliest memories of the sport come from 1998, when he was a seven-year-old boy watching France win the World Cup thanks to two goals by Zinedine Zidane in the final against Brazil!

Kanté became the fourth Chelsea player to win the Football Writers' Association Footballer of the Year award, following on from Gianfranco Zola (pictured receiving the award in 1997 from Sir Stanley Matthews, the first-ever winner), Frank Lampard (2005) and Eden Hazard (2015).

His achievements were also recognised back in his homeland as the French players' union named him the best footballer from France playing abroad. He beat off some quality players to win the award: Karim Benzema, Ousmane Dembele and Antoine Griezmann!

It took Kanté only 72 matches to bring up a half-century of Premier League wins. By the time he reached that figure he'd lost only eight times in the English top flight!

Considering he plays in a team which typically enjoys the majority of possession, for N'Golo to make 127 tackles, which was the second highest in the Premier League in 2016/17, was a fine achievement.

Both of his goals for the club in the 2016/17 campaign were scored against Manchester United.

For over a decade it has been pretty common for fans in this country to call the defensive-midfield position "the Makelele role", named after the ledge that is Claude Makelele during his five years at Chelsea. Now the man himself reckons we should name the position after Kanté! "People talk about the Makelele position, but I am old and it's time everybody called it the Kanté position," he said. "N'Golo deserves that."

The coaches at Leicester City often said they played Danny Drinkwater with Kanté either side of him, such was the distance covered by the energetic midfielder. Eden Hazard agrees with that, saying his team-mate "deserved all the awards he won. It was like playing with an extra man sometimes." And a legendary former Blue also weighed in on the debate with this tweet!

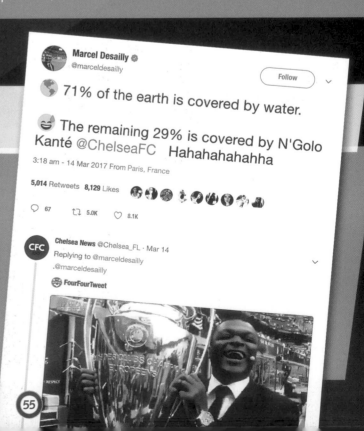

Marcel Desailly @
@marceldesailly
Follow

🌎 71% of the earth is covered by water.

😆 The remaining 29% is covered by N'Golo Kanté @ChelseaFC   Hahahahahahha

3:18 am · 14 Mar 2017 From Paris, France

5,014 Retweets  8,129 Likes

💬 67      🔁 5.0K      ♡ 8.1K

CFC  Chelsea News @Chelsea_FL · Mar 14
Replying to @marceldesailly
.@marceldesailly

FourFourTweet

# PLAYER OF THE YEAR 2017

**Eden Hazard was the star of the show at the Blues' end-of-season awards ceremony, taking home the trophies for Player of the Year and Goal of the Season.**

He became only the second person ever to be voted by fans as our best player in three seasons – the other being club legend Frank Lampard – with the Belgian also winning the prize in back-to-back years in 2014 and 2015.

"Hopefully next year is the same, we win the league and then I win Player of the Year," grinned a delighted Hazard. "Obviously winning the league is what we want most, and this award is just a bonus. We have to be ready every year at the same level to stay at the top."

It wasn't the first time he had scored our Goal of the Season either, receiving that award for the second year running thanks to his amazing dribble through half the Arsenal team to score in the London derby at Stamford Bridge.

"I practise that every day in my garden with my kids," he added. "When I score a goal like that I watch it every day for the rest of the week and then I try to do it again in the next match, but it doesn't work!"

## MR POPULAR

The Chelsea squad had their own ideas about who was our star man of 2016/17, choosing N'Golo Kanté as Players' Player of the Year. The Frenchman must be running out of room in his trophy cabinet, having also won awards from the Premier League, Football Writers' Association and Professional Footballers' Association last season.

## RISING STAR

Mason Mount received the award for our Academy Player of the Year, after the midfielder scored 10 goals in 39 appearances for our development squad and Under-18s, helping the younger age group win every trophy going last season.

## LADIES' CHOICE

The first half of 2017 was also very successful for our women's team, as they won the FA Women's Super League Spring Series, and for the third year in a row the Chelsea Ladies Player of the Year award went to an England international, this time playmaker Karen Carney.

# COMPITITION

**WIN SIGNED CHELSEA SHIRTS!**

We have two shirts up for grabs – a jersey signed by the Blues first team and another signed by the Chelsea Ladies squad. Answer the below questions correctly for your chance to win.

## MEN'S SHIRT

Who scored the winning goal away at West Bromwich Albion which officially sealed our 2016/17 Premier League title?

A) Michy Batshuayi
B) Gary Cahill
C) Willian

Entry is by email only. Only one entry per contestant. Please enter **CFC SHIRT** followed by either **A**, **B**, or **C** in the subject line of an email.

## LADIES' SHIRT

Which England international was named as Chelsea Ladies Player of the Year in 2017?

A) Karen Carney
B) Katie Chapman
C) Fran Kirby

Entry is by email only. Only one entry per contestant. Please enter **CFC LADIES** followed by either **A**, **B**, or **C** in the subject line of an email.

**Joe Plunkett was last year's lucky competition winner.**

In the body of the email, please include your full name, address, postcode, email address, phone number and date of birth and send to: frontdesk@grangecommunications.co.uk by Friday 30th March 2018.

# STADIUM TOUR AND MUSEUM

# VISIT THE HOME OF THE
# CHAMPIONS

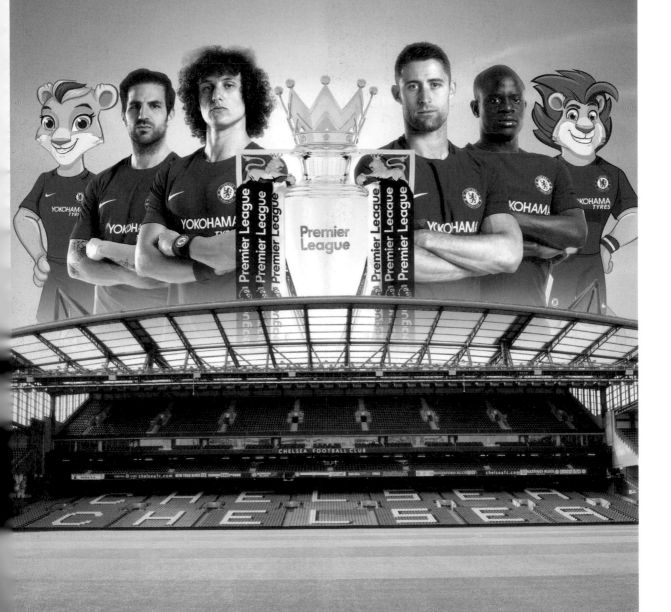

To book, please call **0371 811 1955,**
email **tours@chelseafc.com** or visit **chelseafc.com/stadium-tours**

# STUNNING NEW LOOK FOR THE BLUES

The 2017/18 season marks a new era for Chelsea, with the introduction of the first kits as part of our partnership with Nike.

The home shirt has a modern look while also nodding to the club's proud past. If you ask an older relative about the classic Chelsea kits from the early 1970s, they will tell you about the sides that won the FA Cup and European Cup Winners' Cup for the first time.

This season's home kit has matched the exact shade of blue used on those classic strips and is combined with state-of-the-art technology to deliver a kit fit for champions.

There are many other neat touches, including a round neckline which has "CHELSEA FC" knitted into the back. Both the shirt and shorts feature white stripes down the sides which expand when the player is moving to improve ventilation. "THE BLUES" is written inside the cuff of the right sleeve and the left sleeve features "EST. 1905", referencing the year of the club's formation.

The away shirt and shorts are white with a touch of silver to reflect the huge amount of trophies we have won in recent times, having won every major honour in domestic and European football.

As with the home kit, a mix of technology and club heritage details combine to create a modern strip that feels truly Chelsea.

The 2017/18 home and away kits are available now from www.nike.com/chelsea and in our new Stamford Bridge Megastore.

Turn to page 58 for our exclusive competition to win a brand new home shirt signed by the first-team squad.

Chelsea legend Peter Osgood in our 1971 home kit, which the blue in this season's strip has been based on.

# ANSWERS

## P49 WHEN WE WERE YOUNG

 **A**  **CESC FÀBREGAS**

 **B** **GARY CAHILL**

**C** **DAVID LUIZ**

**D**  **CESAR AZPILICUETA**

**E**  **PEDRO**

**F**  **THIBAUT COURTOIS**

## P50-51 CAPTAIN, LEADER, QUIZMASTER

1) C
2) B
3) C
4) A
5) A
6) A
7) C
8) B
9) C
10) B

## P53 THREE INTO ONE

| **1** | **2** | **3** | **4** | **5** |
|---|---|---|---|---|
|  |  | |  |  |
| LUIZ | CABALLERO | MUSONDA | HAZARD | BATSHUAYI |
| COURTOIS | CAHILL | KANTE | PEDRO | WILLIAN |
| FABREGAS | ALONSO | RÜDIGER | AZPILICUETA | MOSES |

# WHERE'S STAMFORD?

Stamford the Lion and his best friend Bridget the Lioness are celebrating our 2016/17 title win with the rest of the Chelsea fans somewhere in this photo, but can you find them?